# ANGELIC HEALING AND DELIVERANCE GUIDE

## *SUPERNATURAL ENCOUNTERS*

### BY

## APOSTLE OWEN LAWRENCE

OWEN LAWRENCE

# DEDICATION

I specially dedicate this book to my lovely beautiful wife Helen, who was so patient and supportive during the development of this book and to my three wonderful amazing children, Beatrice, prosperity,  Dominionla, for always making me smile, Increase in the wisdom and knowledge of God. I also dedicate this book to all the members of Mount Zion Deliverance & Miracle Centre Int'l. aka Spirit Assembly, for believing in my leadership thank you all more grace in Jesus name Amen.

# TABLE OF CONTENTS

# ACKNOWLEDGMENTS

First I want to thank the almighty God for his grace and wisdom upon my life. I want to thank all those who have been helping and supporting me one way or the other directly or indirectly may God bless you all richly in Jesus name Amen.
Pastor Mrs. Dorothy Osagie, Prophet D  Robert, Pastor Andrew Oloton, Deaconess Mrs. Schola Kevwe Ofuenyi, Mr. Adesotu Stanley Osagie, music films producer, Pastor
Mrs. Osuyi Faith Osadolor, Pastor Nelson Osadolor, Pastor Mrs. Maria Avanrenren, Pastor Lawrence Avanrenren, Evangelist Mrs. Tessy Osas William, Mr. Charlie Avanrenren, Mrs. Judith Edosa, Pastor Athanasius Anyiam, Rev. Andrew Osarumwense Ehigiator, Pastor Ikechuckwu Williams Ifeanyi, Rev. Peter aghahowa.

# DESCRIPTION AND  INTRODUCTION

## Description.

Description and introduction
In this book, you will learn the most strategic ways on, how to use Angels to minister healing and deliverance. You will also learn about Supernatural Encounters of Journey To Heaven Experience.The Deep things of God love, Mercy, and Grace helping Humanity to find peace and comfort of Generational blessings. Introduction
We are living  at a time that is unique in human history. Everyone has an important role or part to play in the work of the final harvest. God is doing all the stuff we read about all over the world remarkable every day events.
The events recorded in this book are not meant to simply entertain anyone. They are meant to serve as a catalyst and inspire you! They are meant to pull you into the deeper things so that you can write your own story of experience! They are meant to deepen your desire for the Lord and His kingdom. The Angelic Healing and Deliverance Guide.Supernatural Encounters are for everyone.

It would be impossible for this book to contain all the testimonies of the people who have God's healing scriptures and miraculously recovered from their physical, spiritual, or mental afflictions. Know this truth: Jesus Christ has conquered disease and death through the power of His Word, His blood, and His holy Name.

The ministry of angels is evident throughout Scripture, which says angels are "ministering spirits sent out to minister to those who will inherit salvation" (Heb. 1:14). As Christians, we should rejoice like the angels when people give their lives to Him and appreciate that there are "innumerable" angels in heaven, and each has an assignment from God (Heb. 12:22).
Angels can also help during deliverance ministry. I became aware of this once while I was in the middle of a deliverance session for

Everyone has angels with them. From the moment you are born, you have at least two guardian angels with you and they will be by your side until you come to the end of your physical life. Nothing you do, say, feel or think can ever make your angels leave your side. The angels are God's messengers and helpers and they see you through the eyes of unconditional love. Their guidance is always gentle and loving. When you desire help from your angels, you simply need to ask in Jesus name, because of the Law of Free Will, the

angels can only assist you when you request their help or if your life is ever endangered. They hear and attend to your requests, whether you call for them out loud or reach out with your thoughts and feelings. They always offer loving guidance to point you in the direction of your dreams and destiny.

# Chapter 1. Angelic Assistance In  Deliverance

It is during these times that we experience a breakthrough from heaven. Often a healing and deliverance angel will come to assist in the work of ministry. The presence of angels in our ministry greatly increases the anointing and like the secret service, they also provide protection.

God used angels to close the mouth of the lions and wage spiritual warfare in the heavens. They can attend to our aid as they did Elijah in 1 Kings 19:5-8 and Jesus in Matthew 4:11 and Luke 23:43

I have seen God's angels at work different times… they are awesome ministering spirits as the Bible says!

Hebrews 1:14, "Are they, not all ministering spirits, sent forth to minister for them who shall be heirs of salvation?"

We can take joy in knowing that angels can help during deliverance ministry and that at the great end-times harvest, angels will be used by God to "gather out of His kingdom all things that offend, and those who do evil and will throw them into a fiery furnace." (Matt. 13:41-42).

A Man from North America last year asking for prayer to find liberation from the evil spirits that have tormented he for years.

My heart broke over the life he had lived — severe abuse, mental torment, Satanism, occult activity, communion with demons, and other evils. The grace of God was extended, in a loving manner, to this Man.

We held a prayer session for him at Mount Zion Deliverance & Miracle Center Graz. The session lasting into the night, we battled the forces of darkness, many evil spirits were cast out — many powerful spirits that resisted (but not for long as God's power overcame their strength).

The demonic powers would place this Man in a trance like a state and demons spoke out of him, often times in a strange voice unlike his (some even growled and acted like an animal). Most of the time his eyes had rolled in the back of his head, we saw only the white — the demon looking at us. It seemed as though we were dealing with stronger spirits.

The evil powers named themselves and gave us the spiritual right they held onto in Man's life. This allowed us to systematically demolish the various strongholds that the demonic beings that built over the years. Glory to Jesus Christ of Nazareth.

The Church stood in their Christ-given authority and earnestly prayed for this Man's deliverance. we battled and battled. But we were not alone — God's Holy angels arrived in the church and assisted us in battle. Allow me to explain…

Often times the demons would completely knock him to the ground (even cause him to crawl around like an animal at times). In each instance, we commanded the angels to pick him up off the ground and in each instance, the angels listened and obeyed our commands. The angels literally, without the aid of any human assistance, picked the body of the Man up off the ground and placing him in a position where we could minister to him. What an awesome display of God's goodness and power! Many angels showed up. The angels assisted in also restraining the demons, binding them, and holding them (as there were a number of times the demons attempted to force the Man outside of the church). In several instances, the demons did cause him to leave the church only for the angels to bring him back in by our commands in the name of Jesus.

What a good God we serve as He allows us to minister alongside His angels for His glory.Many evil spirits were cast out of his body and he was completely set free in the name of Christ, our eternal God.

# Prayer Points for Angelic Assistance in Deliverance

1. LORD, Your angels ascend and descend upon my life; for You have given Your angels charge over me to deliver me in the name of Jesus (Gen. 28:12; Ps.91:11)

2. The angel of the LORD chases and persecutes my enemies in the name of Jesus (Psa. 35:5, 6)

3. Your angels fight for me in the heavens against principalities and powers in the name of Jesus(Dan.10:13)

4. The angel of Your presence saves me and goes before me to make the crooked places straight in the name of Jesus (Isa. 63:9; Zech.12:8)

5. LORD, thank You for sending Your angels to minister to me and before me to prosper my way in the name of Jesus (Matt.4:11; Exod. 33:2)

6.LORD, hear my voice and send Your angels to deliver me from the hand of the enemy in the name of Jesus (Num. 20:16; Matt. 12:11)

7. I have come to Zion; to an innumerable company of angels; LORD, thank You, You confess me before Your Holy Angels (Heb. 12:22; Luke 12:8)

8. I am an heir of salvation, LORD, send Your angels to minister to me by day and in the night in the name of Jesus (Heb. 1:14; Acts 27:23)

9. Your angels meet me as I walk in my destiny in the name of Jesus (Gen. 32:1)

10. LORD, I send out Your angels to be involved in reaching the lost; to gather them in the name of Jesus (Acts 8:26; Matt. 13:41)

11. LORD, I release Your angelic army to fight for and defend Your Church in the name of Jesus (Psa. 68:17).

12. LORD, You have sent Your angels to smite the demons that come to destroy me, my family, ministry, and church in the name of Jesus (Isa. 37:36)

13. I Thank You, Lord Jesus, for this angelic assistance.

## I ministered to another Lady

Who had been looking for the fruit of the womb for many years, pain, anger and sorrow were all blended into the core.

After the demos manifested and  threatened to kill her. When I asked the Father to send a warrioring angel, the Woman  told me she felt something push right up through her stomach. A demon came flying out of the mouth, she vomited out. They were running for their lives.It was an intense war — but the last evil spirit was driven out.Sins were renounced, emotional healing took place, and the lady was instantly healed delivered and set free of various physical and spiritual demonic elements. The LORD has given her two children now,she was completely free

total deliverance from delayed conception by the power in the blood of Jesus.


I pray that God will touch everyone believing on him for the fruit of the womb. God answers prayers, when you do it the right way.

## Prayer Points for the fruit of the womb

1. Blood of Jesus, light the candle of my life and family in the name of Jesus

2. Blood of Jesus neutralize every demonic toxin assigned to kill good seeds in my womb in the name of Jesus

3. Blood of Jesus repair every spiritual and physical damage done to my womb by household wickedness in the name of Jesus.

4. I claim divine healing in every area of my life by the power in the blood of Jesus

5. I cancel every negative medical report issued to me by the power in the Blood of Jesus

6. Blood of Jesus flush out every evil plantation in my body in the name of Jesus.

7. Blood of Jesus fertilize my womb.

8. Blood of Jesus swallow every serpent and scorpion assigned to swallow seeds in my womb in the name of Jesus.

9. Blood of Jesus, quench every strange fire/heat assigned to burn good seeds in my womb in the name of Jesus.

10. Blood of Jesus, come between me and any spiritual spouse coming between me and my fruitfulness in the name of Jesus.

11. Every diagnosed and undiagnosed sickness in my body, be purged by the blood of Jesus.

12. Blood of Jesus change the story of my life to Glory

13. Blood of Jesus overhaul my life in the name of Jesus

14. Blood of Jesus change my trails to testimony in the name of Jesus

# Chapter 2. Angelic Assistance In Healing

The angels of heaven that are assigned to you are now welcoming you to their realm that will take you to a higher level in God. We must embrace the entire realm of His Kingdom. This includes the ministry of angels. Ministering angels are sent to help assist in the work of ministry – every Church should have them!

Are they not all ministering spirits, sent forth to minister for them who shall be heirs of salvation?Hebrews 1:14
For He will give His angels charge concerning you, To guard you in all your ways.Psalm 91:11
Then the devil left Him, and angels came and ministered to Him.Matthew 4:11

Angels are released from God's throne in heaven into the affairs of man. They are involved in all facets of life in both the spiritual and natural everyday activities of man.

We all need healing at various times in our lives. Physical, spiritual, emotional, moral or relationship healing. If you need healing in any area of your life today, listen carefully to God by reading the Bible, by communicating with

him in prayer, by asking God to release his angels to minister healing to you and by seeking godly counsel. Commit to pleasing the Lord, doing things his way. Trust Jesus. God is Jehovah-Rapha, the Lord who heals you.
He said, 'If you listen carefully to the voice of the LORD your God and do what is right in his eyes, if you pay attention to his commands and keep all his decrees, I will not bring on you any of the diseases I brought on the Egyptians, for I am the LORD, who heals you.'" Exodus 15:26

He longs to heal us of resentfulness, bitterness, and pride if we will but trust Him and walk before Him in obedience. Let's allow Him to examine our hearts and heal us of the diseases that sin inflicts upon us.

Angelic Assistance in Healing is a powerful spiritual healing system and levels to bring balance to our entire being a significant improvement in many aspects of our lives.During or after a healing session you may experience the Angels of God sent to minister healing to you. Some people see colors, others feel energies, content, relaxed, and empowered etc. As Kingdom warriors, we can expect to experience angelic activity to be an integral part of the Kingdom life of every Christian. We are now living in the last days where everything is being accelerated. Walking close to God and working with angels is a required mandate for those that desire to be part of the move of God that is now taking place on earth.

## Testimony of Angelic Assistance in  Healing a Sister that came to one of our prayer meeting in the City of Graz Austria .Sister "N"

On February 4th, 2017  a Nurse who had heart pain increasingly worse, after several doctors visit their only help was with pain medicine. She had the pain for several weeks, but it had got progressively worse. The pain is so intense that she can't sleep or rest at all.

At this point her husband really wanting her to go back to the hospital, so she called a friend who told her to consider going to Church healing program, but her husband: "He doesn't easily go to Church.So after a few minutes of talking with her friend, who said she knew our Church was having a program (THEME. My Case is Urgent) and that God had worked greatly through Apostle Owen and several people had been healed in his meetings. Her husband was kind of skeptical, but he couldn't say no and they finally came around.

So I asked if she believed that God could heal her? "Yes," she answered, then I began to pray, two angels were standing in front of me dressed Like Doctor, I asked God to send angels to help heal her, suddenly healing angels assisting and she was Instantly healed.Her testimony is almost unbelievable, God did several miracles,

Plus her husband receiving Jesus as Lord and Savior that was the biggest miracle that will point people to the One true God that loves them.

Only God can do that, I thank God for this family. I pray that God would continue to help them in Jesus name

## Here's another answer to a prayer of  Angelic Assistance in  Healing ministry trip to Nigeria last year.

Many amazing miracles God instantly and perfectly healed using his angels to minister healing to people that came to the Program.

It was difficult to describe the raw emotion of the Holy Spirit at work among us.
I saw the Lord move mightily in many ways and I ministered under a very strong prophetic anointing during the whole trip which was exciting. The Lord gave me a word of knowledge in a few minutes while ministering to people.The Lord said that there was a person  "Champion" for the Kingdom and was going to be used to affect the continent of Africa and the world. I also saw the Lord doing various miracles, including seeing a man who had suffered a stroke was instantly healed. There were many sick people made well and those in pain were given relief. Jesus is still in the miracle business and He says He will "confirm" His Word with signs following. Praise the Lord.

# Chapter 3. Angels and Their Missions

Please Note that it is forbidden to worship or Pray  to an angels

And I John saw these things and heard them. And when I had heard and seen, I fell down to worship before the feet of the angel which shewed me these things. Then saith he unto me, See thou do it not: for I am thy fellow servant, and of thy brethren the prophets, and of them which keep the sayings of this book: worship God.Revelation 22:8-9. Offering our worship or prayer to anyone but God is idolatry.
Prayers can only be granted by someone with omnipotent, omniscient, and omnipresent powers.
Jesus answered him, "It is written, 'YOU SHALL WORSHIP THE LORD YOUR GOD AND SERVE HIM ONLY.'"Luke 4:8

But it's critical to note that despite their myriad amazing attributes, not everything is theirs to do. There is at least one critical thing angels cannot and will not do, which is to witness to the saving grace of Jesus in their own lives.

Angels testify to the glory and creation of God, but God has called you and me to witness of the grace of God.

Bless the Lord, you His angels, Who excel in strength, who do His word, Heeding the voice of His word.Bless the Lord, all you His hosts, You ministers of His, who do His pleasure.Psalm 103:20-21

You are not bothering the angels when you ask God for their help!  They are here to help us shift and change but they need to be invited to help in order to do so. They are always there emotionally supporting us and giving messages but it's not until we ask for their help that they are allowed to step in and intervene in your life. In addition to asking God for an Archangels, you can also ask for the specialty angels. Specialty angels work in different areas to help the world. So whatever you need help with, ask God to send the angel in charge of that  in the name of Jesus

Angels must be sent or release by God or by his children.
I have said, Ye are gods, and all of you are children of the highest."Psalms 82:6.
Herein is our love made perfect, that we may have boldness in the day of judgment: because as he is, so are we in this world.1 John 4:17

One of their missions is to help us with our mission and our life in general. They do this in many ways, Unlike people, as soon as you ask  God for angels assistance, they will help you!  They will also never judge you and are always supportive.
Archangels are a very powerful type of angel, likened to the commanders of armies of angels.They are mentioned specifically in the bible

Aside from guardian angels, they are probably the most well-known type of angels.   So if you are working with or asking  God for  an archangel, know that you are also working with a lot of other angels as well.  Archangels are similar to specialty angels in that they also have areas that they work in or have expertise in but they often have more than one area that they can help us with in the name of Jesus

## Michael the Archangel

Archangel or Saint Michael is a powerful protector and warrior. He is said to have led the battle against the army of fallen angels and he is often depicted in artwork slaying the devil.  His name means "Power of God" and he is powerful!  He can help you if you feel fearful and he can protect you against real or imagined fears.

But the prince of the kingdom of Persia withstood me one and twenty days: but, lo, Michael, one of the chief princes, came to help me; and I remained there with the kings of Persia.Daniel 10:13. Yet Michael the archangel, when contending with the devil he disputed about the body of Moses, durst not bring against him a railing accusation, but said, The Lord rebuke thee. Jude 1:9. And there was war in heaven: Michael and his angels fought against the dragon; and the dragon fought and his angels. And prevailed not; neither was their place found any more in heaven. And the great dragon was cast out, that old serpent, called the Devil, and Satan, which deceiveth the whole world: he was cast out into the earth, and his angels were cast out with him. Revelation 12:7-9

## Gabriel the Archangel

Gabriel is mentioned in the Bible as the angel who came to Mary and announced that she would give birth to Jesus. Gabriel acts as a main messenger between us and heaven and helps us with anything to do with communication whether it is talking, singing, writing etc.

And in the sixth month the angel Gabriel was sent from God unto a city of Galilee, named Nazareth, . To a virgin espoused to a man whose name was Joseph, of the house of David; and the virgin's name was Mary. And the angel came in unto her, and said, Hail, thou that art highly favoured, the Lord is with thee: blessed art thou among women.And when she saw him, she was troubled at his saying, and cast in her mind what manner of salutation this should be. And the angel said unto her, Fear not, Mary: for thou hast found favour with God. And, behold, thou shalt conceive in thy womb, and bring forth a son, and shalt call his name Jesus.He shall be great, and shall be called the Son of the Highest: and the Lord God shall give unto him the throne of his father David: And he shall reign over the house of Jacob forever; and of his kingdom there shall be no end. Then said Mary unto the angel, How shall this be, seeing I know not a man? And the angel answered and said unto her, The Holy Ghost shall come upon thee, and the power of the Highest shall overshadow thee: therefore also that holy thing which shall be born of thee shall be called the Son of God. And, behold, thy cousin Elisabeth, she hath also conceived a son in her old age: and this is the sixth month with her, who was called barren. For with God nothing shall be impossible. And Mary said, Behold the handmaid of the Lord; be it unto me according to thy word. And the angel departed from her. Luke 1:26-38

## Raphael the Archangel

Raphael is an Archangel working in conjunction with Archangel Michael who helps with a whole host of issues.Raphael plays a great role in many different ways.he helped in healing meetings. He can help reduce addictions and cravings and is powerful in healing other injuries and illnesses, with cures often occurring immediately.His name means "Healer of God.

Although the Bible nowhere mentions an angel named Raphael.It is quite possible that the "angel of the pool" the sick man was waiting for was Raphael.

Now there is at Jerusalem by the sheep market a pool, which is called in the Hebrew tongue Bethesda, having five porches.In these lay a great multitude of impotent folk, of blind, halt, withered, waiting for the moving of the water.For an angel went down at a certain season into the pool, and troubled the water: whosoever then first after the troubling of the water stepped in was made whole of whatsoever disease he had. John 5:2-4

He said, 'If you listen carefully to the voice of the LORD your God and do what is right in his eyes, if you pay attention to his commands and keep all his decrees, I will not bring on you any of the diseases I brought on the Egyptians, for I am the LORD, who heals you.'" Exodus 15:26

25

We all need healing at various times in our lives. Physical, emotional, moral or relationship healing. If you need healing in any area of your life today, listen carefully to God by reading the Bible, by communicating with him in prayer,by asking God to release his angels to minister healing to you and by seeking godly counsel. Commit to pleasing the Lord, doing things his way. Trust Jesus. God is Jehovah-rapha, the Lord who heals you.

# Chapter 4. My Journey to Heaven

Dreams visions and encounters are a significant part of what God is doing on the Earth today. If we are willing and aware, God can speak to us in this areas and give us light for our path as well as destiny words for those around us. And afterward, I will pour out my spirit on all people. Your sons and daughters will prophesy, your old men will dream dreams, your young men will see visions. Even on my servants, both men and women, I will pour out my spirit in those days. (Joel 2:28-29) In the year that king Uzziah died I saw also the Lord sitting upon a throne, high and lifted up, and his train filled the temple. Isaiah 6:1

For the most part of the things we encountered or experienced are things concerning our own lives or the lives of those around us. For those who minister a lot, that has a much broader context. All I have experienced for the most part have spoken to me about personal things. For this chapter, I tried to choose the ones that had a broader message that you could benefit from

If we position ourselves before the Lord to receive, we can enjoy this blessing as well. As you read these encounters, ask the Lord to increase this in your life as well.

Very often those of us who pursue the supernatural things of God have an adjustment period when it begins to manifest in our lives. Because we don't start out with any experiential knowledge of things like angelic visitations or trans-relocation or being in the spirit, we relegate such things to "dream" status. No matter what we really experience, we believe at first that it is some sort of dream rather than some sort of spiritual reality. Things will become more apparent of what they truly are the more we experience them. As we experience things more and more, we become more aware and can engage the deep things of God more fully.

## My Journey.

In the season of pondering how best to pursue God and the supernatural life in Him, then I engaged in Fasting and Prayer almost all night Prayer I desired and the Lord visited me in this way. 2005  sometime during the night, I awoke in the spirit realm. I found myself in a very spacious gate or area of some sort and the atmosphere around me was alive. I just kind of looked around in amazement like you (I) normally do in these situations. At this point, the atmosphere around me was most-like and surrounding someone in front of me. As my eyes adjusted, I saw a very tall Man, his body was white and transparent at these time I perceived he is an angel.

The angel that guards the Gates of Heaven told me that, before anyone is received into heaven where they would reside for eternity with God he/she must have or possessed an immortal body, that flesh and blood cannot enter, because God is an immortal spirit. Immediately my body was changed into immortal body shining white as light like the angels that talked with me, then I finally enter into heaven.The thoughts that passed rapidly through my soul in that moment of amazement Is the originality and  truthfulness of everything in heaven
An abounding joy at being thus brought into a glory of the brightest hopes. It was, indeed, good to be thus carried, as it were, into Paradise, or the third heaven, and to hear their words which human lips might not reproduce.

Let's see some practical examples from the Bible and from life experiences of God kingdom glory. Peter, James, and John.This would give them an idea of the glory prepared for them when changed by his power

## Condition to enter Heaven.

After six days Jesus took with him Peter, James, and John the brother of James, and led them up a high mountain by themselves. There he was transfigured before them. His face shone like the sun, and his clothes became as white as the light. Just then there appeared before them Moses and Elijah, talking with Jesus.

 Peter said to Jesus, "Lord, it is good for us to be here. If you wish, I will put up three shelters—one for you, one for Moses and one for Elijah." While he was still speaking, a bright cloud covered them, and a voice from the cloud said, "This is my Son, whom I love; with him, I am well pleased. Listen to him!" When the disciples heard this, they fell facedown to the ground, terrified. Matthew 17:1-6

There was a man of the Pharisees, named Nicodemus, a ruler of the Jews: The same came to Jesus by night, and said unto him, Rabbi, we know that thou art a teacher come from God: for no man can do these miracles that thou doest, except God be with him. Jesus answered and said unto him, Verily, verily, I say unto thee, Except a man be born again, he cannot see the kingdom of God. Nicodemus saith unto him, How can a man be born when he is old? can he enter the second time into his mother's womb, and be born? Jesus answered, Verily, verily, I say unto thee, Except a man be born of water and of the Spirit, he cannot enter into the kingdom of God.That which is born of the flesh is flesh, and that which is born of the Spirit is a spirit. Marvel not that I said unto thee, Ye must be born again.The wind bloweth where it listeth, and thou hearest the sound thereof, but canst not tell whence it cometh, and whither it goeth: so is every one that is born of the Spirit.Nicodemus answered and said unto him, How can these things be?Jesus answered and said unto him, Art thou a master of Israel, and knowest not these things? Verily, verily, I say unto thee, We speak that we do know, and testify that we have seen, and ye receive not our witness.If I have told you earthly things, and ye believe not, how shall ye believe, if I tell you of heavenly things? And no man hath ascended up to heaven, but he that came down from heaven, even the Son of man which is in heaven. And as Moses lifted up the serpent in the wilderness, even so, must the Son of man be lifted up: That whosoever believeth in him should not perish, but have eternal life. John 3:1-15

## I saw many things in heaven, I asked many questions and I learn many things

I saw many things in heaven. There are many angels who look like human beings, but their bodies are transparent you can easily see through them, they do not have wings, I also saw some group of angels who have wings. The amazing thing about them is that they can appear and disappear, they can pass through the wall. I saw the street the Bible talk about streets of gold very beautiful many flowers with different colors that are not on the Earth. I saw many big beautiful mansions Jesus talk about in the Bible it is true, some of the building walls are built with gold. I saw some group of angels that sing and some with trumpets the trumpets look like an elephant Longhorns or animal Longhorns the trumpet color look like gold, but they were all putting on shining white clothes. When they begin to sing the atmosphere increase with the glory of God, they have an amazing voice. The angels that took me around showing me many things. He took me to my house, I have a house in heaven, my house is very beautiful, even the walls of my house is made of gold. I was just like a king, I have many angels around me, who served me drinks. Heaven is a very busy place, People, and angels everywhere, Then I saw the throne of the almighty God,  the throne was filled with light, I could not look so much at it, because of the lights, but I saw someone sitting on the throne. When you get to heaven you will only see one person, when you ask where is the Father the person will say  I am,  when you ask where is the Son the person will say I am, when you ask where is the Holy Spirit the one person will say I am. I was very happy to meet my glorious father your father Our Father what a joy. The atmosphere of the presence of the Lord is very strong someone can be

electrified by the atmosphere, I felt it all over me. From Heaven, They showed me the picture and the video of hell, I saw so many people crying shouting screaming help help help Inside the Fire. Then the Lord said to me that is where I save you from my son. I was told that anyone that is not safe he or she is already in hell, that is why we need to tell everyone the good news about the Lord Jesus Christ the savior so that we can save them from hell.

## These are some Bible references.

There are also celestial bodies, and bodies terrestrial: but the glory of the celestial is one, and the glory of the terrestrial is another.1 Corinthians 15:40.

In my Father's house are many mansions: if it were not so, I would have told you. I go to prepare a place for you. John 14:2
If you had known Me, you would have known My Father also; and from now on you know Him and have seen Him."Philip said to Him, "Lord, show us the Father, and it is sufficient for us."Jesus said to him, "Have I been with you so long, and yet you have not known Me, Philip? He who has seen Me has seen the Father; so how can you say, 'Show us the Father'? John 14:7

Whoever believes in Him is not condemned, but whoever does not believe is already condemned, because he has not believed in the name of God's one and only Son. John 3:18

When I woke up from this great encounter my body was filled with the glory of God when people come closer to me or  If I touch them, they will be shaken or fall down, because of the glory of God that  I saw in heaven, Was manifesting physically,it was all over me if they had any sickness or disease they will be healed Instantly.

I remember an event that happened during this time a friend of mine was having a program, he invited me to the program, but I was not the guest speaker. during the service, He asked me to lead the prayer session, I did not prepare any way, as I took the microphone  to pray My eyes open I saw the scripture in the air.Psalm 34:7 The angel of the Lord encamps around those who fear him,and he delivers them. As I began to read the scripture angels where  ascending and descending from heaven, Some of them carry something like a  box of gift.

Everywhere was filled with the angels of the Lord and the glory of God filled
the service everybody was falling down  including the ministers, they could
not stand the glory of God nobody could stand, even me I was also shaking I
could not stand as well,but the best part of it is. Everybody was deliver set
free from whatsoever disease or sickness they had. Everyone was happy and
everybody was looking at me, but I knew it was the glory of God that I saw in
heaven  is manifesting even in the physical. Hallelujah glory be to God
Almighty for his glory.

## These are some Bible references.

So that the priests could not stand to minister because of the cloud: for the glory of the LORD had filled the house of the LORD.1 Kings 8:11

And he dreamed, and behold a ladder set up on the earth, and the top of it reached to heaven: and behold the angels of God ascending and descending on it.Genesis 28:12

Then He declared, "Truly, truly, I say to all of you that you will see heaven open and the angels of God ascending and descending on the Son of Man."John 1:51

This is the message we have heard from Him and announce to you, that God is Light, and in Him there is no darkness at all.1 John 1:5

But we all, with open face beholding as in a glass the glory of the Lord, are changed into the same image from glory to glory, even as by the Spirit of the Lord. 2 Corinthians 3:18

Blessed be the Lord, who daily loadeth us with benefits, even the God of our salvation. Selah.Psalm 68:19

I would like to stop here for now if you want to learn more please look out for my new book title. The language of God secret of creation, how to say it and see it happening. Thank you and God bless.

# Chapter 5. The Spoken Words and Commanding Power

Death and life are in the power of the tongue, And those who love it will eat its fruit." Proverbs 18:21

If anyone does not stumble in word, he is a perfect man, able also to bridle the whole body. Indeed, we put bits in horses' mouths that they may obey us, and we turn their whole body. Look also at ships: although they are so large and are driven by fierce winds, they are turned by a very small rudder wherever the pilot desires. Even so the tongue is a little member and boasts great things. See how great a forest a little fire kindles! And the tongue is a fire, a world of iniquity. The tongue is so set among our members that it defiles the whole body, and sets on fire the course of nature; and it is set on fire by hell. For every kind of beast and bird, of reptile and creature of the sea, is tamed and has been tamed by mankind. But no man can tame the tongue. It is an unruly evil, full of deadly poison.

With it we bless our God and Father, and with it we curse men, who have been made in the similitude of God. Out of the same mouth proceed blessing and cursing. My brethren, these things ought not to be so. Does a spring send forth fresh water and bitter from the same opening? Can a fig tree, my brethren, bear olives, or a grapevine bear figs? Thus no spring yields both saltwater and fresh." James 3:1-12

For assuredly, I say to you, whoever says to this mountain, "Be removed and be cast into the sea,' and does not doubt in his heart, but believes that those things he says will be done, he will have whatever he says." Mark 11:23

# SPEAK BLESSINGS, NOT CURSING

We, as fallen humans, have a natural tendency to do evil rather than good, due, of course, to the nature of sin which is incarnated in us. We have almost always the capacity to curse others more than we have to bless them, especially those that have hurt us one way or another.
If we want to be happy and healthy we must learn from the Holy Spirit to obey and please God rather than our flesh. We need to acquire the habit of speaking blessings all the time no matter how challenging the circumstances may be at the present moment. A person who speaks blessings seems always to be healthier and happier than those who always begin their day cursing, hating and meditating in the lies of the devil. Stop saying negative words throughout the day, learn to say positive ones. Learn to bless yourself and other people.

Early 2006 I was conducting a meeting on deliverance in the city of Benin, Nigeria. A woman came up to me asking for
prayer. When I laid my hands on her a demonic force began to manifest. The woman was totally controlled by a demon who began cursing and saying he had jurisdiction in her life because her
mother had given her to him. After about 30 minutes of deliverance prayer the demon left her and she became conscious again. That woman was about 38 year old unmarried, she told us that she began having spiritual
problems when she was at the age of 7. She told us that her mother hated her and used to curse her by saying that she belonged to the devil. In doing that, the mother simply gave Satan the right to possess the daughter.

We need to be careful with the type of words we are speaking to others, especially to our children because we have authority over them. Depending on what we say we can transfer this authority over to Satan and he is going to be the one who will have control over our children,

spouses, relatives, friends, etc. Curses produced by spoken words in one's life will always be a hindrance for healing, prosperity, peace, and all the good things you desire. Once detected, the curse must be broken in order for the person to receive God's blessings.

Always remember that life and death are in the power of the tongue, and those who love it will eat its fruit.

## Attracting blessing or cursing

Anyone who opposes God and his people attracts curse.
I will bless those who bless you, and whoever curses you I will curse; and all peoples on earth will be blessed through you."
Genesis 12:3.
After the defeat of Jericho, Joshua declared, "Cursed before the LORD.
And Joshua adjourned them at that time, saying, Cursed be the man before the LORD, that riseth up and buildeth this city Jericho: he shall lay the foundation thereof in his firstborn, and in his youngest son shall he set up the gates of it.
Joshua 6:26
Joshua's curse was literally fulfilled years later during the reign of King Ahab.
We read in 1 Kings 16:34, "In his days Hiel of Bethel built Jericho. He laid its foundation at the cost of Abiram his firstborn, and set up its gates at the cost of his youngest son Segub, according to the word of the LORD, which he spoke by Joshua the son of Nun."

First, Joshua clearly did not want to see this city that worshiped other gods to be rebuilt. A curse was upon its citizens and their memory due to their worship of false gods.

Second, the destruction of Jericho served as an example to other cities that opposed Israel and its God. When the Israelites crossed the Jordan River, Jericho was the first major city they encountered. Its devastation would serve as a powerful warning to other people in the land of God's power.

Third, Joshua realized the negative influence the city could have on the Israelites.
Joshua's curse served many purposes, yet one of the most significant was the exact fulfillment of the curse hundreds of years later. That is the power of spoken words and command

All families have traits or characteristics that are passed down from generation to generation. There are physical and spiritual traits that are passed down from generation to generation, including blessings and curses. You'll see a mom and a daughter who look almost exactly alike; you'll see a father and his son who is the spitting image of him. There are also traits like depression, divorce, alcoholism, drug addiction, infirmity, anger or perversion to name a few.

I want you to know there are also family spirits, or familial spirits that pass down from generation to generation. For example a spirit of perversion can manifest things like lust, adultery, fornication and molestation. Incest is certainly a generational and/or a family curse. How many of us know our grandparents on both sides of our family? How about our great grandparents or our great great grandparents? We don't know them, and we have no idea whether or not they loved God or if they hated Him.

In 1 Samuel 3:12-14 it gives the curse on Eli saying,

"In that day I will perform against Eli all that I have spoken concerning his house, from beginning to end. For I have told him that I will judge his house forever for the iniquity which he knows, because his sons made themselves vile, and he did not restrain them. And therefore I have sworn to the house of Eli that the iniquity of Eli's house shall not be atoned for by sacrifice and offering forever. I'd sure hate to be in that family line, wouldn't you?

Now, most folks who want to argue this point will say something like, "Well, that's Old Testament! Show me one in the New Testament." So, I refer them to Matthew 27:22-25, which gives the curse spoken by the nation of Israel concerning Jesus' death.

"Pilate said to them, 'What then shall I do with Jesus who is called the Christ?' They all said to him, 'Let Him be crucified!' Then the governor said, 'Why what evil has He done?' But they cried out all the more saying 'Let Him be crucified!' When Pilate saw that he could not prevail at all, but rather that a tumult was rising, he took water and washed his hands before the multitude, saying, 'I am innocent of the blood of this just Person. You see to it.' And all the people answered and said, 'His blood be on us and on our children.

David, the man after God's own heart, fell into sexual sin with Bathsheba. He committed adultery and then had her husband Uriah murdered to cover up his sexual sin. As a result we see a history of incest, rape, rebellion and womanizing in his children. You always reap what you sow, it's a spiritual law!

There is good news to go along with this. That good news is found in Gal 3:13, one hung on a tree to take our curses upon Him. Jesus paid a full price on Calvary! In Acts 2:21 says, "And it shall come to pass that whoever calls on the name of the Lord shall be saved. Meaning escape, deliverance, healing, to rescue, redeem, reclaim and salvation.

The precious blood of Jesus not only paid for our sins, but it also paid for our healing and our deliverance. This includes the breaking of generational curses. But, the blood must be applied to break the curse.
So, let's look at how we apply the blood to break these generational curses. First, we must confess our sins and the sins of our ancestors.

After we confess our sins and the sins of our forefathers and foremothers we then renounce the curses and break them. I prefer to break them by name if possible. An example of this would be:
I repent of my sins and the sins of my forefathers and foremothers in the area of addiction back to the 3rd, 4th, even the 10th generation and beyond. I renounce and break every generational curse of addiction in my family on my mother's side and my father's side. I break it past, present and future from this moment on, in Jesus Name! Amen!

## Breaking Curses and Releasing the Blessings Prayer Points

1. I am redeemed from the curse through the blood of Jesus (Galatians 3:13).
2. I am the seed of Abraham, and his blessing is mine (Galatians 3:14).
3. I choose blessing instead of cursing and life instead of death (Deuteronomy 11:26).
4. I break and release myself from all curses on both sides of my family back sixty generations.
5. I break and release myself from all generational curses and iniquities as a result of the sins of my ancestors in the name of Jesus.
6. I break and release myself from all curses of pride and rebellion in the name of Jesus.
7. I break all curses of witchcraft, sorcery, and divination in the name of Jesus.
8. I break and rebuke all curses of sickness and infirmity in the name of Jesus.
9. I break and release myself from all curses of death and destruction in the name of Jesus.
10. I break and release myself from all curses of poverty, lack, and debt in the name of Jesus.
11. I break and release myself from all curses of double-mindedness and schizophrenia in the name of Jesus.
12. I break and release myself from all curses of rejection in the name of Jesus.
13. I break and release myself from all curses of Jezebel and Ahab in the name of Jesus.
14. I break and release myself from all curses of divorce and separation in the name of Jesus.

15. I break and release myself from all curses of lust and perversion in the name of Jesus.

16. I break and release myself from all curses of wandering and vagabond in the name of Jesus.

17. I break and release myself from all curses causing accidents and premature death in the name of Jesus.

18. I break and release myself from all curses of idolatry in the name of Jesus.

19. I break and release myself from all curses of confusion and mental illness in the name of Jesus.

20. I break and release myself from all spoken curses and negative words spoken against me by others and by those in authority, and I bless them.

21. I break and release myself from all self-inflicted curses by negative words I have spoken in the name of Jesus.

22. I break and release the grudges and hatred that have been passed down from previous generations.

23. I break all evil affiliations from previous generations, we break altars erected to other gods in past generations from my maternal and from my paternal side.

24. From this day on, we dissociate from all affiliations with anything that is contrary to your will.

25. I command every demon hiding and operating behind a curse to come out in the name of

## Testimony of a Sister that came to one of our prayer meeting in the City of Graz Austria

## Sister "B"

I knew I wanted deliverance. I didn't know how or when, but I was determined God was going to change these areas in my life. God led me to seek deliverance from these Ministry Team MZDMC. It was a very difficult time for me. The Lord started uprooting things from my past, including molestation as a child, and perversion growing up as well as the fear, anger, and hatred of men that were results of these past hurts and abuses. During the day I would be fine, nothing ever bothered me at all. But as soon as I shut my eyes to sleep, either sexual thoughts, or fear would come into my mind. It was so bad that I couldn't sleep, and during the night I would feel pressure on my chest and heart and almost couldn't breathe and a voice would tell me I was going to die. I didn't' tell anyone about my struggles because I felt ashamed and dirty.

When I went through deliverance I would get uncomfortable and want to leave, but I stayed, and Jesus set me free from fear, control, and perversion! Praise the Lord for the freedom he has given me and the peaceful sleep he has blessed me with.

I now know who I am in Christ. The devil doesn't' want Christians to know who they are in Christ. I can also minister to other people now. The team spoke the truth to me, I received it, and the truth set me free.
The first thing we should take care of in the prayer meeting is to be punctual. The meeting life is a help to the spiritual life of a Christian; it is also an expression of the Body.The prayer meeting is the best test of our spiritual power.

Let me tell you the story of a Man who came to me few years ago asking for prayer. He began telling me his story. I was  involved in a car accident four years ago,the doctors have tried their best and i have been in pain for 4 years straight.
I  am crippled one leg shorter than the other one.
I want to take care of my children and  my wife." While he  was talking, the three children and his wife were crying. My heart was filled with compassion. As I asked
him to sit in a chair in the middle of the prayer room, I noticed that he had a very serious problem in his back, it was totally crooked. his foot was also crippled and crooked, One leg was shorter than the other. In fact, he told me that
he was embarrassed to be around friends because of his condition.
Immediately after praying for him, he said , i felt the presence of God all over me. I  am now completely healed, completely free, and completely joyful glory be to God.

# Chapter 6. Lying is devil end time tools

Lying is a huge issue for many people, including Christians

The devil is so good at lying that many of God's glorious angels did not detect his deceit nor understand his manipulative schemes. The devil is a genius and among created beings he has no equal in the universe. When people in positions of trust and respect promote his lies as truth, they especially honor Lucifer. Lucifer was the first liar and with his lies he deceived one-third of Heaven's angels a minimum of 200 million angels while living in God's house.

Revelation 12:7-9  And war broke out in heaven: Michael and his angels fought with the dragon; and the dragon and his angels fought,  but they did not prevail, nor was a place found for them in heaven any longer.  So the great dragon was cast out, that serpent of old, called the Devil and Satan, who deceives the whole world; he was cast to the earth, and his angels were cast out with him.

A liar is a person who doesn't speak the truth. A lier is a person or object that rests in a horizontal position.lie" can also refer to misleading or inaccurate.

A big lie which attempts to trick the victim into believing something major which will likely be contradicted by some information the victim already possesses, or by their common sense. When the lie is of sufficient magnitude it may succeed

It is the communication of a false statement that harms the reputation of an individual person, business, product, group, government, religion, or nation.Other various kinds of defamation.

One may deny a lie made on a previous occasion, or one may alternatively claim that a previous lie was not as egregious as it actually was. For example, to claim that a premeditated lie was really "only" an emergency lie, or to claim that a self-serving lie was really "only" a white lie or noble lie does not necessarily have to be a complete fabrication. While a lie is related by a speaker who believes what is said is false, offered by a speaker who does not care whether what is said is true because the speaker is more concerned with giving the hearer some impression. Thus may be either true or false, but demonstrates a lack of concern for the truth which is likely to lead to falsehoods.

Most of us tell more than one lie per day.We lie all the time, despite the fact that it costs us considerably more mental effort to lie than to tell the truth. It is also difficult to spot a misleading "fact" when we hear something that on the face of it, sounds true.The facts do not tell the whole truth.be aware that what you think is the truth may very well be deceptive.

The serpent deceived  Eve.
Satan's plan was to draw our first parents to sin, and so to separate between them and their God. it was Satan's policy to enter into talk with her when she was alone. There are many temptations to which being alone gives great advantage; but the communion of saints tends very much to their strength and safety. Satan took advantage by finding her near the forbidden tree. They that would not eat the forbidden fruit, must not come near the forbidden tree. Satan tempted Eve, that by her he might tempt Adam.
2 Corinthians 11:3
I am afraid, however, that just as Eve was deceived by the serpent's cunning, your minds may be led astray from your simple and pure devotion to Christ.

It is his policy to send temptations by hands we do not suspect, and by those that have most influence upon us. Satan questioned whether it were a sin or not, to eat of this tree. He did not disclose his design at first, but he put a question which seemed innocent. Those who would be safe, need to be shy of talking with the tempter. He quoted the command wrong. He spoke in a taunting way. The devil, as he is a liar, so he is a scoffer from the beginning; and scoffers are his children.

John 8:44 You belong to your father, the devil, and you want to carry out his desires. He was a murderer from the beginning, refusing to uphold the truth, because there is no truth in him. When he lies, he speaks his native language, because he is a liar and the father of lies.

It is the craft of Satan to speak of the Divine law as uncertain or unreasonable, and so to draw people to sin; it is our wisdom to keep up a firm belief of God's command, and a high respect for it. Has God said, Ye shall not lie, nor take his name in vain, nor be drunk,it is well said; and by his grace we will abide by it. It was Eve's weakness to enter into this talk with the serpent: she might have perceived by his question, that he had no good design, and should therefore have started back. Satan teaches men first to doubt, and then to deny.
Genesis 3:3
but from the fruit of the tree which is in the middle of the garden, God has said, 'You shall not eat from it or touch it, or you will die.'" Genesis 3:4  And the serpent said unto the woman, Ye shall not surely die:

Despite the fact that we now frequently expect lies from those in power, it remains challenging to spot them in real time, especially by politicians,  estate agents, bankers and journalists.
Unfortunately, the prevalence of lies might stem from the way we are brought up. Lies play a role in our social interactions from a very young age.

How different with men than with God. Men, with the exception of some cases, do not even consider lying a crime and hardly a sin. We speak or at least think of deception as a way of life; we call deception a "little white lie." We almost expect dishonesty. When we don't want to talk to someone on the phone, we don't tell them the truth; we may have our secretary tell them we "are not in." Now when it comes to money and material things, then we start taking these sins seriously, in fact we call them crimes. And the more money or possessions are involved, the more severe the crime and its punishment.

The story of Ananias and Sapphira, recorded at the beginning of Acts chapter 5. This couple had committed no crime, but they had committed a sin. They had not stolen money, nor extorted it, nor embezzled it. They had simply kept a part of that which was theirs. They must have kept back only a small portion of it, but in so doing, they had lied. And for this, they died.

I can see this backdrop as fitting into the situation of Ananias and Sapphira quite directly. Others were selling their possessions and giving all they made from them to the apostles to meet the needs of poor brethren. I assume that people were selling their extra possessions and property, not their own dwellings. The property they were selling was their security, their "nest egg," that which assured them that there would be provisions for the future.

Ananias and Sapphira may well have said to themselves, "If we sell all that we have, we will have nothing to fall back on." Keeping back a little of the money they obtained from the sale of their property would give them a little security, they must have reasoned. And, so long as they were honest in their dealings, it would have been their right to do so. But in order to carry this off, and to look as "spiritual" as the others, they had to lie, saying they were giving their all when they weren't. They were, in the process of providing for themselves, not trusting in God, and they were not obeying His commandments, for they were lying. No wonder this could be called "putting the Spirit of God to the test."

Example of mask lie
Consider the estate agent who tells a potential buyer that an unpopular property has had "lots of enquiries" when asked how many actual bids there have been. Or the used car salesman who says a car started up extremely well on a frosty morning, without disclosing that it broke down the week before. Both statements are true but mask the reality of the unpopular property and the car. It happens because we constantly have so many competing goals.We want to achieve our narrow objective – selling a house or car – but we also want people to see us as ethical and honest.

But why is lying such a serious offense to God? Why was this deception, which seems to have hurt no one, so drastically disciplined by God? I think the answer is quite evident: the church is founded upon truth, and it grows by means of truth. The unity of the church is also dependent upon truth.

Deception is an attack on the truth, and it is also one of the primary means of attack employed by Satan, the liar and deceiver. To tolerate even a small deception is to open the door to an attack on the truth which would be devastating.

Men put God to the test when they doubt His provision and when they act independently, when they act disobediently, seeking to provide for themselves in their own way.

When our Lord was tempted by Satan, He had been in the wilderness, without food for 40 days Matthew 4:2; Luke 4:1-2. Satan sought to induce Jesus to act independently, indeed, disobediently, seeking to produce what He wanted His own way, rather than obeying the Father and waiting for Him to produce what He had promised, in His own way and in His time. Specifically, Satan suggested that Jesus leap from the pinnacle of the temple, based upon God's promise of protection. Jesus refused, based on the fact that this would be to "put God to the test" and thus would be disobedience to God.

Taking all these factors into consideration, it seems to me that men are inclined to put God to the test in the area of God's provisions—specifically food. God has promised to provide, and He has called upon men to obey His commands and to wait upon Him to provide in His time.

## Prayer to overcome deception

1. Father, by Your divine grace I will not be deceived. I will not accept the lies of the enemy that are against You and against Your Holy Commandments; against the truth about who Jesus Christ is: God in human form, Lord and Savior, born of a virgin, died on a cross, who on the 3rd day was physically and gloriously raised from the dead. He is King, King of Kings and Lord of Lords. He is my Lord. He is my Savior.

2. Dear God in Heaven, I will not accept the lies of the enemy against my own soul, against my own life and against my better judgment. I reject all forms of deception that the enemy has tried to sow into my own heart from childhood to this point in my life

3. You have given me the Spirit of Truth, the Holy Spirit. He will lead me and He will guide me away from error into all truth. I am a sheep of your pasture. Your sheep hear your voice and the voice of a stranger I will not follow.

4. Thank you, God, for giving me wisdom and discernment in these last days to not only lead my life but to lead my family, to lead my spouse and to lead my children in the ways of justice, truth and righteousness.

57

5. I am fearfully and wonderfully made. I am loved by God, called by God, chosen by God, anointed by God and appointed by God for such a time as this. My life counts. My life matters. I have a purpose.

6. I come against every lie that has tried to find a home in my thought life, in my mind, in my heart, and in my soul and I reject it in Jesus' name. I receive the truth of what the Word of God declares me to be. I am a child of God.

7. I have a future and I have a destiny that I must fulfill through the grace of the Lord Jesus Christ and the power of the Holy Spirit. I will remain true to the word of God and the teachings of scripture In Jesus name Amen.

# Chapter 7. How to Minister Healing and Deliverance

Throughout the gospels we see that in many occasions and situations Jesus spoke out loud to the problems people faced, whether they were infirmities or evil spirits, the fact is that Jesus spoke and gave orders. He commanded eyes to be open, evil spirits to come out, lame to walk, deaf to hear, dead to rise up, fever to go away, hand to be restored, etc. We as His ambassadors on earth need to come up to the surface and exercise the authority He has given to His church on earth (Luke 10:19). We need to represent Jesus with humility, authority and determination. We are called to serve Jesus with passion, boldness, obedience and holiness as well. We are His ambassadors on earth. We, then, are called to change what is wrong and make it right in the Name of Jesus Christ, our Lord.

The most effective way to heal someone is by speaking to the problem the person is facing. Speak out loud. The devil who is holding someone captive will only obey you if you step up to the plate and command him to come out in the mighty Name of Jesus Christ. If it's cancer then speak to the spirit of cancer. If it's aids then give the spirit of aids a command to leave the person's body in the name of Jesus Christ. If it's cigarette addiction then command the spirit of nicotine to come out in the name of Jesus Christ. If it's migraine headache then speak out loud and command that spirit to go in Jesus Christ's Mighty Name. Speak to the problem as if it were to a person, in fact, diseases and infirmities are result of influence and works of evil spirits in humans.

According to the Bible, the challenges and battles we face aren't always medical or natural in nature. On the other hand, the Bible is just as clear that all of the struggles we confront in life are certainly not demonic or supernatural in nature either. Jesus clearly recognized the difference between physical disease and maladies, deformation, epilepsy, and spiritual demonic bondage (Matthew 4:23–24). He successfully healed all of the above without apparently deferring to one over the other.

Jesus was going throughout all Galilee, teaching in their synagogues and proclaiming the gospel of the kingdom, and healing every kind of disease and every kind of sickness among the people. The news about Him spread throughout all Syria; and they brought to Him all who were ill, those suffering with various diseases and pains, demoniacs, epileptics, paralytics; and He healed them.

We know it is possible to treat many physical challenges, mental disorders, and chemical imbalances without resorting to blaming spiritual warfare and demonic spirits. We should be just as aware that the New Testament reveals there are some physical, mental, and emotional problems that actually can have a supernatural cause. These may be specifically supernatural in origin or also have a natural explanation (Luke 8:26–29, 13:10–11). Then they sailed to the country of the Gerasenes, which is opposite Galilee. And when He came out onto the land, He was met by a man from the city who was possessed with demons; and who had not put on any clothing for a long time, and was not living in a house, but in the tombs. Seeing Jesus, he cried out and fell before Him, and said in a loud voice, "What business do we have with each other, Jesus, Son of the Most High God? I beg You, do not torment me." For He had commanded the unclean spirit to come out of the man. For it had seized

him many times; and he was bound with chains and shackles and kept under guard, and yet he would break his bonds and be driven by the demon into the

desert. "Jesus asked him, saying, 'What is your name?' And he said, 'Legion,'because many demons had entered him."
(Luke 8:26–30)

Say out loud, "evil spirits, I bind you in the name of Jesus Christ, my savior. I rebuke you and command you to come out of (person's name). I rebuke you spirit of leukemia, come out of (person's name) and never enter him/her again, in Jesus' mighty name. I command you spirit of aids, come out of (person's name) and enter him/her no more, in Jesus Christ's name. Spirit of diabetes, I command you now come out of (person's name) in Jesus' name and enter him/her no more. Spirit of epilepsy, I rebuke you and command you to come out of (person's name) in Jesus' mighty name. Spirit of sexual perversion I rebuke you in Jesus' mighty name, come out of (person's name) and enter him/her no more. Whatever the problem may be this is how you should pray. Always speak out loud to whatever "mountain" needs to be removed or cast out, be bold and persistent, speak with authority in the mighty name of Jesus Christ.

The Bible states that the "thief comes only to steal, and to kill, and to destroy." John 10:9. Demons not only can place diseases in human bodies, but they also can control our minds to force us to follow their instructions, for an example, they can easily manipulate people to make them have poorly diets, drink alcoholic beverages, smoke cigarettes, take drugs, etc. In many cases you only can get rid of diseases through the discerning of the works of the devil. Once they are detected in someone's life then it will be easier to set that person free. You only can successfully help people to be set free from diseases if you understand that demons and diseases are related to each other. In fact our struggle is not against flesh and blood.

I believe demons attach themselves through breaches in our soul through hurt disappointment fear and lines of inequity.Its a door that needs to be closed. I find addictions are just the way our soul tries to comfort itself,which brings in demonic strongholds.
ask God to show you areas of your life (soul)which may still need healing and forgive all that has hurt you or disappointed you even yourself and God. If this is a pattern in your family it is a line of inequity

Also the bible says that demons are
always looking for "houses" to live in, and those houses are human bodies.
"When an unclean spirit goes out of a man, he goes through dry places, seeking rest; and finding none, he says, 'I will return to my house from which I came.'" Luke 11:24
"…and certain women who had been healed of evil spirits and infirmities-- Mary called Magdalene, out of whom had come seven demons." Luke 8:2

There are some practical ways that helps accelerate the process of faith in us, for example: reading the Bible--understanding God's ways toward us, praying without ceasing (1 Thessalonians 5:17), fellowship with people of strong faith, avoid hanging out with folks of negative attitude, avoid cursing others, and learning to confess God's promises.

intensive prayer session, especially if the prayer
warriors target the spirits by rebuking them and casting them out in Jesus' name. The power that is in the name of Jesus will by default eliminate the power of that particular spirit who's holding the person captive, and so forth.

If our concern is truly the well-being of those entrusted to our care, then we must have the integrity, security, and courage to send people where they are likely to receive effective help, regardless of how this affects our pride. Sometimes that help will come from a medical doctor. At other times, the immediate need may be a good marriage or family counselor. There are also occasions where the best help available is in the office of a local pastor.

# Chapter 8.The Components Process of Healing and Deliverance

Jesus went throughout Galilee, teaching in their synagogues, preaching the good news of the kingdom, and healing every disease and sickness among the people." Matthew 4:23. When the even was come, they brought unto him many that were possessed with devils: and he cast out the spirits with his word, and healed all that were sick: Matthew 8:16.

In the healing and deliverance process there are some components that I consider
important, they are present in the Bible and were seen during Jesus healing and deliverance, ' ministry. Their application are not important just for healing and deliverance, but also for
other areas of our life. Some of them are motivated by love, and some by faith. These components include the following: hope, desire, patience, prayer, love, joy, faith, command, expectation, determination, petition, action, confession and perseverance. They are all interrelated to each other and when put into practice they work in a powerful way.

Let's see some practical examples from the Bible and from life experiences as well as the results of the application of some of these biblical components in the
healing process. Mark 5:24-34—"A
large crowd followed and pressed around Him. And a woman was there

who had been subject to bleeding for twelve years. She had suffered a great deal under the care of many doctors and spent all she had, yet instead of getting better she grew worse. When she heard about Jesus, she came up behind Him in the crowd and touched His cloak, because she thought, 'If I just touch His clothes, I will be healed.' Immediately her bleeding stopped and she felt in her body that she was freed from her suffering. At once Jesus realized that power had gone out from Him. He turned around in the crowd and asked, 'Who touched my clothes?' 'You see the people crowding against you,' His disciples answered, 'and yet you can ask, "Who touched me?"' But Jesus kept looking around to see who had done it. Then the woman, knowing what had happened to her, came and fell at His feet and, trembling with fear, told Him the whole truth. He said to her, 'Daughter, your faith has healed you. Go in peace and be freed from your suffering.'" Let me ask you something. What do you think motivated that woman to keep searching for healing without giving up? Just a simple desire to be made whole. She had a deep desire to become a normal person. Her desire generated perseverance and action--during 12 years she went from place to place and from doctor to doctor searching for healing without giving up. Finally, when she heard about Jesus she was determined and single-minded. She knew in her heart that this was the opportunity of a lifetime. The moment had arrived and once again she took action to go after Jesus with single-minded determination to be healed. She set a condition for herself: "If I touch His clothes I will be healed . . ." Her faith was based on that condition, but her determination would not accept failure. She knew what she wanted and she got it.

Let's look at another example of God's

power in conjunction with some of the key components. Mark 1:40-42 - "A man with leprosy came to Him and

begged Him on his knees, 'If you are willing, you can make me clean.' Filled with compassion, Jesus reached out His hand and touched the man. ' I am willing,' He said. 'Be clean.' Immediately the leprosy left him and he was cured." In this short passage we see some of the components being put into action. For example, the man with leprosy came to Jesus. It means he took ACTION by going after Jesus. he had DESIRE to be made whole. he had HOPE to find a cure for his body. When he saw Jesus he EXPECTED to receive healing. He BEGGED (asked) Jesus on his knees. "Filled with COMPASSION, Jesus reached out His hand and touched the man. 'I'm willing, 'He said. 'Be clean!' (COMMAND) Immediately the leprosy left him and he was cured." And JOY sealed the process. It is amazing how effective

Jesus was in His ministry. It is important for us to know that the power of God is still as available to us today as it was to Jesus 2000 years ago. His power is available through the person of the Holy Spirit, through the name of Jesus, through the Bible, and through you and me, because Jesus gave us authority to trample on snakes and scorpions and to overcome all the power of the enemy (Luke 10:19). As I mentioned before, these key components are interrelated. They begin with desire and end with faith. Love and compassion are also important ingredients in this process, never despise them.

# Chapter 9. Generational Blessing

God expects righteous parents to leave an inheritance for their children – II Chron. 12:14. Parents need to pray and work towards being a blessing and leaving an inheritance for their children. Generations unborn are waiting to benefit from your existence on earth. The primary reason why God prospers His people is to empower them to establish His kingdom.

A word spoken with some particular form of spiritual power and authority for good or evil that sets in motion something that will probably go on from generation to generation.

Our God is a generational God. When He created Adam, he spoke to him about his seeds. To Abraham, he spoke about his seeds even when it seemed a physical impossibility to have a child at age 75 – Gen. 1: 28; 3:15; 12:1-3. When God blesses, he expects it to be extended to future generations and when he curses, it is also generational except something is done about it! Gen. 3:15-16; Exod. 1:9; 20:5-6; Gen. 8: 20-22. For instance, God began with Abraham in Gen. 22:15-18; 26:1-5, shifted to Isaac's generation Gen. 28:1-6, Jacob and his generation Gen. 41: 37-46; and to the fourth generation – Joseph Exodus 3:16.

Are you ready to stand up for a thousand-generation blessing on your family? You might even include others outside your family in these prayers of faith.

This might be one of your finest hours.
Spiritual blessings. (Deu 7:9 ) Know therefore that the LORD your God is God; he is the faithful God, keeping his covenant of love to a thousand generations of those who

The prophet Ezekiel talks about a time when God's people ran after sin instead of God. God didn't want to punish them but, "I looked for someone among them who would build up the wall and stand before me in the gap on behalf of the land so I would not have to destroy it, but I found no one." (Ezekiel 22:30)

I think parents have a special place in the spiritual history of their kids and grandkids. Are you standing against the enemy in prayer and faith? Are you grabbing hold of God's promise of blessing for them?

Others have grown children. Sometimes it looks like they are making choices that pull them away from God's blessings. Can't we stand between them and the destruction that the devil wants for them?

Now, I know that sociologically, families pass on traits—good and bad. And we still must deal with this heritage in our life. But, in Christ, we're no longer a prisoner! We can grow into something better.

I bless my family for a thousand generations! My kids, my grandkids, their kids, on and on into the future. Make our family a blessing. If the world is still standing a thousand years from now let my family be blessed and blessing others in Jesus' name.

In this prayer he reminds God of the promise made to Abraham of the blessing belonging not to him exclusively but also to his seed,

## PRAYER POINTS

1. I acknowledge the almighty power of God that saves to the uttermost and delivers from all forms of bondage. Father, continue your reign in my life forever.

2. Father, I repent of my shortcomings, rebellion and unguarded utterances which the devil might want to use to accuse me before you. In Jesus' name, cover me with your grace and mercies.

3. Every evil power wanting to pollute and corrupt my generational blessings is rendered impotent in the name of Jesus.

4. The rod of the wicked shall not rest upon my life in the name of Jesus.

5. Every struggle of the enemy against my destiny, look back to your defeat at the cross. You have failed over me in Jesus' name.

6. By the blood of the Lamb, I declare that Satan has no authority over me and my loved ones in Jesus' name.

7. Any way the devil might have tampered with my destiny, let the fire of the Holy Ghost restore in the name of Jesus.

8. Father, this life of mine is to fulfill a purpose of glory. I have not come into this world in vain. In Jesus name, I will fulfill my purposes in life; I will reach my goals; I will fulfill a destiny of glory.

9. I refuse to handover spiritual and physical liabilities to my children in the name of Jesus.

10. Let the blood of Jesus cleanse my lineage of all idolatrous and adulterous practices.

11. In Jesus' name, I revoke, cancel and annul the effects of my ancestors' ungodly choices, invocations, actions and declarations over my life and children.

12. Father, I lay hold on father Abraham's blessings, bless me in the village, bless me in the city. Let the dew of heaven drop on my laps with the fatness of the earth in Jesus' name.

Thank you so much for reading this book may you be blessed and increase in wisdom and the knowledge of God.May you receive angelic visitation and Supernatural Encounters.May you be healed and delivered in every area of your life.May you be blessed and be a blessing to your generation in Jesus name Amen.

# ABOUT THE AUTHOR

# APOSTLE OWEN LAWRENCE

Apostle Of Wealth Distribution. A visionary and provocative thinker, Global Business Microfinance Consultant, the CEO of OMBFC, the Founder and Senior Pastor of MZDMC, anointed preacher, calling as an Apostle.mentor, author, professional trainer, entrepreneur, Financial Coach, A global humanitarian doing charitable work to help the needy, A heart of compassion to the hurting, message of freedom and empowerment to the oppressed and disenfranchised.

www.owenlawrence.site

olaw2007@yahoo.com